Go to sleep litue

Close your pretty .... eyes
Time for little Darling baby
To go to sleep

All the lullabies in *Hush-a-bye Baby* are also
available on a delightful musical cassette

Also by Ian Beck

EMILY AND THE GOLDEN ACORN
THE TEDDY ROBBER
THE TEDDY ROBBER miniature edition

Hush-a-bye Baby

A First Book of Lullabies

Chosen by Carolyn Fickling   Illustrated by Ian Beck

PICTURE CORGI BOOKS

HUSH-A-BYE BABY
A PICTURE CORGI BOOK 0 552 52656 8

First published in Great Britain by Doubleday,
a division of Transworld Publishers Ltd

PRINTING HISTORY
Doubleday edition published 1990
Picture Corgi edition published 1992

Picture Corgi Books are published by Transworld Publishers Ltd,
61–63 Uxbridge Road, Ealing, London W5 5SA, in Australia by
Transworld Publishers (Australia) Pty Ltd, 15–23 Helles Avenue,
Moorebank, NSW 2170, and in New Zealand by Transworld Publishers
(N.Z.) Ltd, 3 William Pickering Drive, Albany, Auckland.

Printed in Belgium by Proost

For Susy Upton I.B.
For Daniel Fickling C.F.

Contents

Rock-a-bye Baby

Rock-a-bye baby,
On the tree top,
When the wind blows,
The cradle will rock,
When the bough breaks,
The cradle will fall,
Down will come baby, cradle, and all.

Evening

Hush, hush, little baby,
The sun is in the west,
The lamb in the meadow,
Has laid down to rest.

The bough rocks the bird,
The flower rocks the bee,
The wave rocks the lily,
The wind rocks the tree.
And I rock the baby so softly to sleep,
She must not awaken,
Till daisy buds peep.

What Shall We Do With Baby-o?

What shall we do with baby-o,
What shall we do with baby-o,
What shall we do with baby-o,
If he won't go to sleepy-o?

Wrap him up in calico, calico, calico,
Wrap him up in calico,
Send him to his mummy-o.

Wrap him up in a table-cloth,
Throw him in the fodder loft.

Tell your daddy when he comes home,
And give Old Blue your chicken bone.

Dance him north, dance him south,
Pour a little moonshine in his mouth.

Baby Beds

Little lambs, little lambs, where do you sleep?
In the green meadow with mother sheep.

Little birds, little birds, where do you rest?
Close to our mother in a warm nest.

Baby dear, baby dear, where do you lie?
In my warm bed with mother close by.

Gaelic Cradle Song

Hush the waves are rolling in,
White with foam, white with foam.
Father toils amid the din,
But baby sleeps at home, at home.

Hush the winds roar hoarse and deep,
On they come, on they come.
Brother seeks the lazy sheep,
But baby sleeps at home, at home.

Hush the rain sweeps o'er the ewes,
Where they roam, where they roam.
Sister goes to seek the cows,
But baby sleeps at home, at home.

How Many Miles to Babylon?

How many miles to Babylon?
Three score and ten.
Can I get there by candlelight?
Yes and back again.
If your heels be nimble and light,
You may get there by candlelight.

Maggoty Pie

Hush-a-bye baby,
The beggar shan't have 'ee,
Nor more shall the maggoty pie.
The rook nor the raven,
Shan't take 'ee to Heaven,
So hush-a-bye baby bye bye.

Sleep, Baby, Sleep

Sleep, baby, sleep,
Your father tends the sheep.
Your mother shakes the dreamland tree,
And softly fall sweet dreams for thee,
Sleep baby sleep.

Sleep, baby, sleep,
The large stars are the sheep.
The little stars are the lambs, I guess,
And the gentle moon is the shepherdess,
Sleep, baby, sleep.

Sleep, baby, sleep,
Down where the woodbines creep.
Be always like the lamb so mild,
A kind, and sweet, and gentle child,
Sleep, baby, sleep.

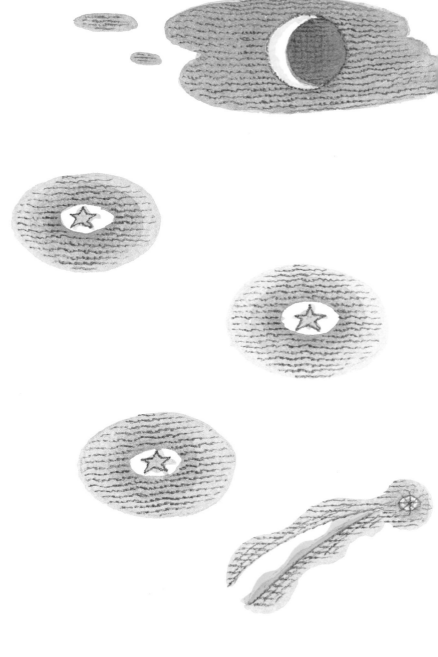

Sleepy Song

Hush-a-bye baby,
Daddy's away,
Brothers and sisters,
Have gone out to play,
But here by your cradle,
Dear baby I'll keep,
To guard you from danger,
And sing you to sleep.

Twinkle, Twinkle Little Star

Twinkle, twinkle little star,
How I wonder what you are,
Up above the world so high,
Like a diamond in the sky.
Twinkle, twinkle little star,
How I wonder what you are.

When the blazing sun is set,
When the grass with dew is wet,
Then you show your little light,
Twinkle, twinkle all the night.
Twinkle, twinkle little star,
How I wonder what you are.

Then the traveller in the dark,
Thanks you for your tiny spark,
He could not see which way to go,
If you did not twinkle so.
Though I know not what you are,
Twinkle, twinkle little star.

Rockin' Horse Lullaby

Rockin' horse cowboy,
Time to go to bed.
Rockin' horse cowboy,
Rest your weary head.
You've been riding hard all day,
Time for you to hit the hay.

Bye Baby Bunting

Bye Baby Bunting,
Daddy's gone a hunting,
Gone to fetch a rabbit skin,
To wrap poor Baby Bunting in.

Bye Baby Bunting,
Mother's gone a milking,
Sister's gone a silking,
Brother's gone to buy a skin,
To wrap the Baby Bunting in.

A Spell for Sleeping

Seven fish in the sway of water.
Six candles for a king's daughter.
Five sighs for a drooping head.
Four ghosts to gentle her bed.
Three owls in the dusk falling.
Two tales to be telling.
One spell for sleeping.

Mocking Bird

Hush, little baby, don't say a word,
Papa's going to buy you a mocking bird.

If the mocking bird won't sing,
Papa's going to buy you a diamond ring.

If the diamond ring turns to brass,
Papa's going to buy you a looking-glass.

If the looking-glass gets broke,
Papa's going to buy you a billy-goat.

If that billy-goat runs away,
Papa's going to buy you another today.

John Boatman

Call John the Boatman,
Call, call again.
For loud flows the river,
And fast falls the rain.

John is a good man,
And sleeps very sound,
His oars are at rest,
And his boat is aground.

Fast flows the river,
So rapid and deep,
The louder you call him,
The sounder he'll sleep.

Brahms' Lullaby

Lullaby and goodnight,
In the sky stars are bright.
Round your head flowers gay,
Scent your slumbers till day.

Close your eyes now and rest,
May these hours be blest.
Go to sleep now and rest,
May these hours be blest.

German Slumber Song

Go to sleep and good night,
In a rosy twilight,
With the moon overhead,
Snuggle deep in your bed.
God will watch, never fear,
While Heaven draws near.

Go to sleep and good night,
You are safe in the sight,
Of the angels who show,
Christmas trees aglow.
So to sleep, shut your eyes,
In a dream's Paradise.

Day and Night

By day the shadows slip away,
At evening back they creep.
The sun gives light enough for play,
The stars enough for sleep.

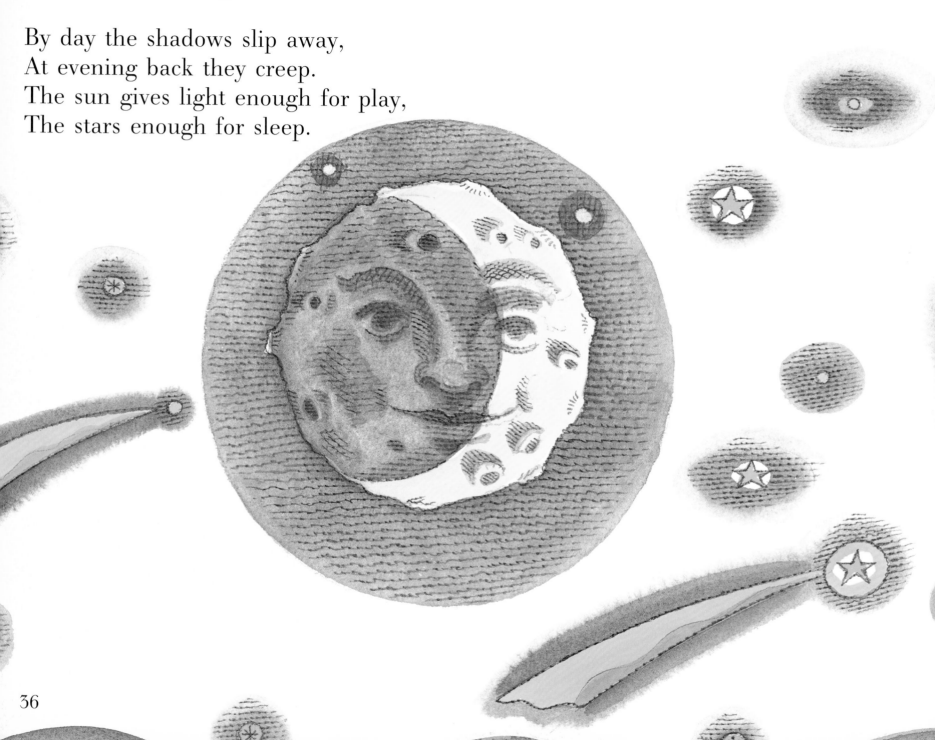

Hush-a-bye Baby

Hush-a-bye baby,
Pussy's a lady,
Mousie has gone to the mill,
And if you don't cry,
She'll come back by and by,
So hush-a-bye baby lie still.

All Through the Night

Sleep my child and peace attend thee,
All through the night.
Guardian angels God will send thee,
All through the night.
Soft and drowsy hours are creeping,
Hill and dale in slumber sleeping.
I my loving vigil keeping,
All through the night.

Golden Slumbers

Golden slumbers kiss your eyes,
Smiles await you when you rise.
Sleep little baby,
Don't you cry,
And I will sing a lullaby.

Care you know not, therefore sleep,
While over you I watch do keep.
Sleep little baby,
Don't you cry,
And I will sing a lullaby.

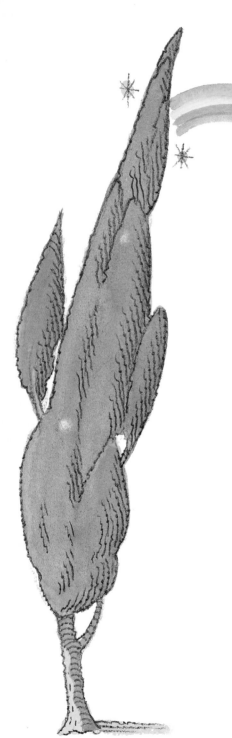

Far in the Wood

Far in the wood you'll find a well,
With water deep and clear.
Whoever drinks by moonlight bright,
Will live a thousand year.

And all around the little well,
Are seven lovely trees.
They rock and sway and sing a song,
And whisper in the breeze.

And through the seven lovely trees,
The evening wind will blow,
And down fall seven little dreams,
My baby all for you.

Oh My Baby

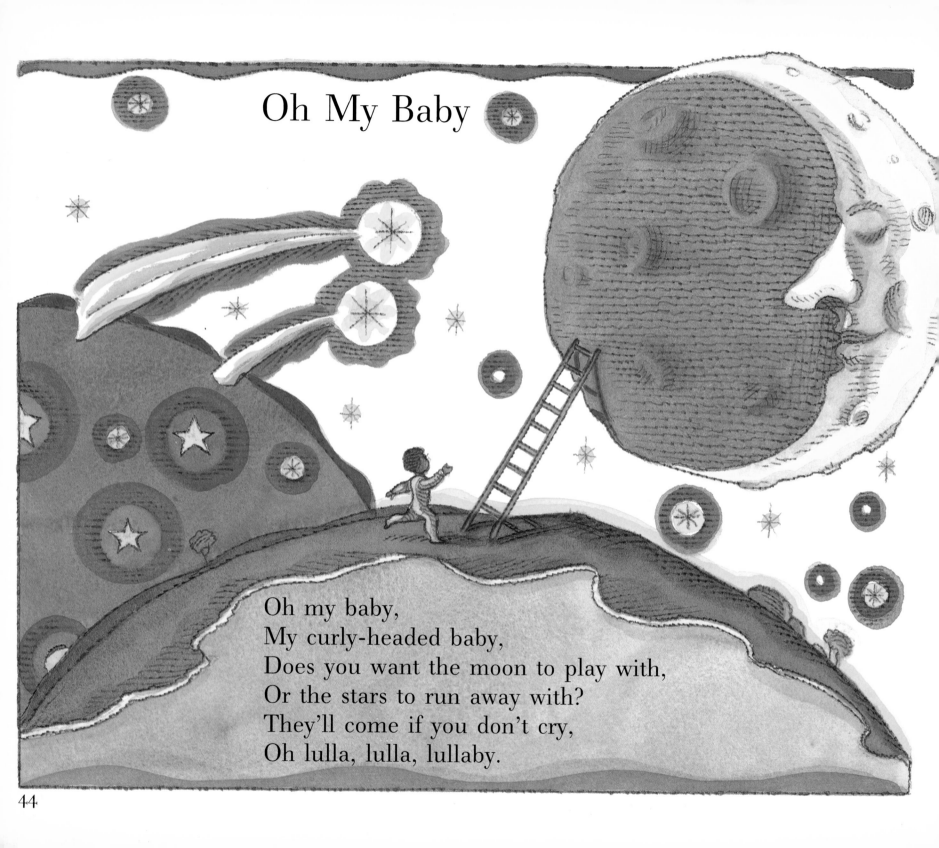

Oh my baby,
My curly-headed baby,
Does you want the moon to play with,
Or the stars to run away with?
They'll come if you don't cry,
Oh lulla, lulla, lullaby.

The Fairy Lullaby

You spotted snakes with double tongue,
Thorny hedgehogs, be not seen;
Newts and blind-worms, do no wrong;
Come not near our fairy queen.

Philomele, with melody,
Sing in our sweet lullaby;
Lulla, lulla, lullaby; lulla, lulla, lullaby!
Never harm,
Nor spell, nor charm
Come our lovely lady nigh;
So goodnight, with lullaby.

Weaving spiders, come not here;
Hence, you long-legged spinners, hence!
Beetles black, approach not near;
Worm nor snail, do no offence.

Philomele, with melody,
Sing in our sweet lullaby;
Lulla, lulla, lullaby; lulla, lulla, lullaby!
Never harm,
Nor spell, nor charm
Come our lovely lady nigh;
So goodnight, with lullaby.

The Fairy Lullaby

Goodnight

Here's a body — there's a bed!
There's a pillow — here's a head!
There's a curtain — here's a light!
There's a puff — and so goodnight!